T0146777

Still

Inspired by God

Maureen Millar

BALBOA.
PRESS

A DIVISION OF HAY HOUSE

Balboa Press books may be ordered through booksellers or by contacting:

Balboa Press
A Division of Hay House
1663 Liberty Drive
Bloomington, IN 47403
www.balboapress.com
1 (877) 407-4847

Because of the dynamic nature of the Internet, any web addresses or links contained in this book may have changed since publication and may no longer be valid. The views expressed in this work are solely those of the author and do not necessarily reflect the views of the publisher, and the publisher hereby disclaims any responsibility for them.

The author of this book does not dispense medical advice or prescribe the use of any technique as a form of treatment for physical, emotional, or medical problems without the advice of a physician, either directly or indirectly. The intent of the author is only to offer information of a general nature to help you in your quest for emotional and spiritual well-being. In the event you use any of the information in this book for yourself, which is your constitutional right, the author and the publisher assume no responsibility for your actions.

Any people depicted in stock imagery provided by Thinkstock are models, and such images are being used for illustrative purposes only. Certain stock imagery © Thinkstock.

Print information available on the last page.

ISBN: 978-1-5043-2963-7 (sc)
ISBN: 978-1-5043-2965-1 (hc)
ISBN: 978-1-5043-2964-4 (e)

Library of Congress Control Number: 2015904117

Balboa Press rev. date: 05/19/2015

Still

Still - without motion or sound, calm, tranquil, quiet.

In the bustle of our day to day life it is often difficult to find the stillness where we hear God's voice. If we are to hear from Spirit we need give Spirit opportunity. It is not that Oneness of the universe isn't in touch with us, encouraging and upholding us, but that we are oblivious.

Your author does not do well with loud noises, negative energies, and flashing lights; so TV is never on, the CD player is rarely used, ring tones are muffled and angry people are kept at bay. I am hyper-sensitive to my environment so keep things low key. Instead, I enjoy the purring of my cat, the chortles of grandson, gentle conversations and the call of the ravens over this rural area in which I dwell. I am retired, living on an island, puttering in the garden, delighting in the countryside and able to spend time alone with the God I know and love. Here I find time and opportunity to jot down the thoughts Spirit imparts. As you read these words and view nature, may you enjoy the touch of nature and vivacity of life which these pages may bring. However do not stop there. Find your own quiet corner, find opportunity to listen to the same still voice, write down the thoughts that reach your heart. Be honest in questioning, authentic in response, mulling kindly the interpretations you find. May God bless you, and all of us. Amen

This book is for those who embrace truth, love, and kindness. Blessings to all.

About the Author

The author is a retired primary school teacher who has enjoyed a relationship with the Spirit of God for many decades in diverse settings. Spirit visits with love, good intentions, and wise words as God/Father/Mother/Sister/Brother/Cousin/Friend.

Maureen leads a quiet but interesting life. Not at all boring, but filled with friends, family, laughter, dancing, cooking, and occasionally painting.
When she takes the time to find a place where it is still and pays attention and is open to instruction, the energy she knows as God, joins her. In this stillness she listens to what is impressed upon her. Without distraction and in peace, she makes handwritten notes of the messages. At another time they are typed and arranged.

Because she thought it not fair to keep all the writings to self, she sought a way to publish the thoughts so that you, too, would be blessed. May these pages always bring you peace, love and a sense of well-being. Amen
Maureen's first book, *Inspired by God*, is available: www.amazon.com/dp/0986779202, she can be e-reached at InspiredbyGod@shaw.ca.

Dedication

This book is dedicated to all those who are searching for truth and knowledge and who are willing to seek spiritual help from the spiritual source we may know as Great Spirit, Holy Spirit, Buddha, Mohamed, Father, Mother Earth, or God.

Together may we find the peace, righteousness and wisdom needed to restore goodness and kindness to the physical realm by seeking answers from our guides and spiritual friends gone before us, who keep close watch upon all, and who cheer us on as we grow and learn.

May we evolve as those who serve, who demonstrate good and holy living. May we be patient as we seek the divine - administering love and courage, helping where we can, cheering gladly when we witness progress. May we learn to work with the harmony of Spirit, and with natural spiritual laws.

Let us use wisdom and reason in all that we do, or refrain from doing. May love, light and truth reign, comfort and knowledge prevail.

A New Day Begins

A new day begins,
New hope appears.
Light and love within and without are unlimited.

Truth waits.
Joy erupts.
Long suffering is held at bay.

I smile,
I soak up sunshine and spread it around,
Even when there's none to be found.

Life is good.
Even the parts that seem harsh are perfectly
ordered. Therefore will I be of good cheer.

A Few Moments

Just a few moments of my day
Can mean a lot to those who come my way,
Even as my heart's made glad
When another smiles, winks, engages me.

When we connect as individuals of a larger
plane Spirits are lightened - yours and mine.
We may see self as but a speck
in space and time.
But we can be bright, welcoming, aglow, kind.

Or a 'wet rag' who doesn't engage with the soul
Of one who needs kind word or deed,
Of one, perchance, who'll send a ray
Of hope and love that meets our need.

Choice begins as I awake to each new day;
I get a fresh start - even if I flubbed it yesterday.
And so do you, if you 'flubbed it' too....
For that, Jesus, we thank you.

A Song on My Lips

God, you have put a song on my lips,
Love in my heart,
Wisdom in my speech.
I thank you.

My steps are light,
My worries few,
Your goodness overwhelms me.
I thank you.

From my heart joy erupts.
Gratitude spills from within.
And everywhere the energy we be
Comforts and sustains me.

Oh God, my God your grace is mine,
Your love is evident,
Your Spirit is a light
That from my eyes can shine.

Acceptance of One Another

Greet one another in love.

Acceptance is a critical component of love.

Accept one another as they 'are',

Whether they're filled with anger, hatred or joy,

Whether disgruntled, greedy or kind.

Be not judgmental.

Love swallows judgment.

It regards favorably.

It receives unconditionally,

And welcomes with positive intention.

Be a channel for love.

Nurture and uphold.

Adversity

Even in the face of adversity remain pure and holy. Take 'the hit' rather than succumb to wayward plans.

Allow Spirit to weave for you a path and a way whereby you will harm none, nor be harmed.

When adversity leaves and once again clear wholesome days arrive, give thanks, give alms, give from the heart to the heart of another who is perhaps now meeting head on the with adversity that visited you.

Some say, "If it doesn't kill you it will make you stronger." Yes, you will become stronger and you will be a model for others.

And in time you will give witness to the truth 'There is No Death'. But in the meantime go by faith and in the Spirit simply rest.

Be blessed and a blessing
Amen.

All is Well

I've been there, where you are, in
frustration, furry, pain; in disbelief,
disgruntled, yet hoping just the same.

I've known confusion, troubles and lack;
these all fade away as I look back and see from
whence I came.

I've been taken to a high place, to heaven and
beyond, past the stars into dimensions new,
not influenced by time or gravity, have you?

No I wasn't high on drugs – I never do the stuff;
but I was showered with a dance of light and
colour which captivated mind and soul.

I tried to join the energy but was sent back
home – accompanied by love – not left alone.
I brought back the excitement of the opportunity.

Brought back too,
the peace I found, and the tranquility.
*All is well, and will be as I in due
course become one with divinity.*

Angels Watch Over Me

Angels surround my bed.
They reach out to bless, caress,
Or welcome home.
These spirit friends watch over me,
Set the stage for who I hope to be,
And to the 'me' that I become.

They lead - but never press,
Give assurance or a needed word,
See me through each day.

I welcome them.
I heed the things they say.
I thank them for the dreams they send
which come my way.

Apology to God

I awoke to a beautiful day. 'God', I said, 'I have no pressing commitments. Today I'm going to spend the day with you.'

But by lunchtime I had spent no time with God. The phone had been ringing, I'd had to follow up with errands and call backs, the dogs needed attention, and my grandson had arrived at the top of the stairs.

I apologized. 'Sorry, God, I didn't get to you.' I really wanted to, and I meant to, but you can see if just didn't happen.'

'Whoa. Whoa a minute' Spirit replied. 'Wasn't I with you in those calls? In the radiant smiles of your grandson. Didn't I wash the floor with you and reorganize the shelves? Treat the dogs to bones and help you find that missing item?

I am with you. There is nowhere you go, no thing you do that excludes me. We are one, you and I, one. We are at one with all life – not only with those things you would consider to be alive, but at one with rocks, the sea, sun, rain, thoughts, intentions and hope.

Be of good cheer. I had a great morning with you. I loved the geese through your eyes, embraced your daughter-in-law with your arms, and corrected the harsh interpretation that one was giving of another with your keen forthrightness.
Keep up the good work. I love hanging out with you.'

Father/Mother/Sister/Brother/Cousin/Friend, thank you. Thanks for being with me always.

Be Big

Be as big as you be!

The 'you' you be, stretches to infinity,
infinity and back again
touching many on its way.

Allow others to explore
and to experience the lessons learned,
the peace you find in this time and in this place.

Currently you vibrate at a reasonable rate
but wait and see how grand you'll be
when life explodes for all to see.

Radiate, already, the magnificence you are,
the wisdom you've become,
the largeness of your heart.

Do not hide in the background
nor flaunt the grandness that's within
but humbly touch those drawn to you.

Stretch their limits, feed their needs;
implant love, hope and kindness.
Grant others the grace you'd like to receive.

Give them Spirit, reason to believe
they're included, accepted by you.
They are welcomed and they are magnificent too.

Be of Gentle Intention

Tread not with heavy foot
upon the land;
Be light and of gentle intention.
Lift up the globe, lift into peace.
Lift unto joy and kindness.

Bless. Do good.
See honestly the expected fulfilling
of your desire for Earth.
Experience unfolding of wisdom
fair treatment
and magnificence.

It is by your intention that you are judged
Not by what transpires.
Therefore keep a watch on what you think.

Choose thoughts clean and righteous.

Be of Good Cheer!

We have known dis-ease, discouragement,
an unknown future.
That's behind us now.
Ahead lies knowing, understanding,
wisdom anew.

We'll find wellness, gladness and truth.
Embraced by the light, coddled with care,
we are refreshed by Spirit and of good cheer

Love springs from within
Hope clings to our mind
Soon we'll have a new story to share.

We'd like to read it when it appears.

Amen

Be Resilient.

Be resilient. Move past anxiety and worry.
Try, with intent.

Put wholehearted energy into a new
direction of your choosing.

Recognize the strength within.
Appreciate what is given to you.

Give thanks.
And give to those whom you can bless.

Be Set Loose

Our feet will not always cling to earth;
Nor will we strive forever.

When we are ready
We'll be set loose to glories
That as yet we imagine not.

Be humble.
Be generous.
Welcome change.
Grasp the gold ring of life and living.
Live life!
Love life!
Be both life and love.
Amen

Be Spirit

Continue in friendliness,
Compassion,
Kindness.
And love.

Be open to praying,
Listening,
Writing,
Speaking.
Dwelling on what's good and pure.

I am willing and able.

Therefore be at peace,
Enjoy these requirements:
Be Spirit.
Be God.

The doors of heaven will be opened.
You will be gifted with peace,
understanding and wholesomeness.

You are and will be
a beacon of light to those who seek
a comfort to those who find,
the steady post one clings to within a storm.

So be it. Amen

Be There

Enjoy the playfulness of puppy at your feet
and puppy's bouncy yipping in your ear.

Resonate, with cat upon your lap,
and with the gentle purring that you hear.

Know who needs a smile, who a word or two,
who some human contact, who a breath of air.

Be there, really be there,
Be there for a while.

When harbored anger erupts,
or emotional pains appear, live life,
Be really there.

If overwhelming joy, or great sadness appears
Live life – be really there.
If a cautious turn of mind comes near, be there.
Grasp, hold close – with no fear.

Believe with Me

My God is not gender specific
Nor does s/he sit upon a throne.
Does not make pronouncements
Or harshly judge.

My God is love, kindness, wisdom.
Energy in motion,
The all-in-all vibration who waits always.
Never despairs.

Who sees for each gladness, growth,
Freshness of Spirit
And a satisfying, expected end.
Not an end as ending...

But an end which leads to new beginning,
Where, on unique path, we continue,
Or take flight in dimensions
Yet to be known.

Bend. Don't Break

Despondent?
Discouraged?
Disheartened?

It's time to seek out gladness.
Watch for opportunity to give thanks.

Experience joy in small successes.
See adversity as occasion for growth.

Bend, don't break.
Whisper, don't shout.
Replace the frown with a smile.
Soon we'll find gladness has been resurrected.

Blessed with Abundance

We are blessed with abundance,

A cup that overflows,

A life which nurtures us

And those around.

Ever are we loved.

Always do we love.

So it is,

And so it shall continue

Till time departs

The sky is rolled away

And alone

I stand before my God.

Blues? Why Should I Worry?

Why should I worry?

Why should I cry?

All that I need

Is close by.

Why should I worry?

Or be in despair?

What I need is here in my heart.

It's here.

I'll look afresh,

I won't whine.

I'll look up

And there encounter God's design.

Change Is on the Horizon

Do I have a skin that I must shed?

A cocoon from which I'll crawl?

Must I weave anew a nest
or find a hole to call my home?

Will the shadow of my God
Watch over me and keep me safe?

And will I find protection
'Neath God's feathered wings?

Spirit answers, 'Yes'.
Wait on me and you will find
Love, Joy, and Perfect Peace.

Yes!

Close the Door

Close the door to the world.
Enter the Kingdom of Heaven.
Here you are at peace;
Here one with Oneness,
One within the All-in-All.

This is not an extravagant hallway,
Nor chapel made of stone.
This is a corner
Where you and God can be alone.
This is a spot older than time
But just as modern as the moment you are in.

Breathe deeply,
Let cares fall away.
Calm Spirit,
God is with you, here, today.
Listen. Contemplate. Explore.
And 'be', simply, be.
Be, once more.

Amen.

Come on Over

Come on over to tranquility.
Come 'home'
To a kind and gentle spirit
That greets you as its own.

Let the stillness of this moment
Sink deep within your soul
Be loved, refreshed, at peace -
Made whole.

Stay here for awhile
Be comforted; dwell within this space.
Be at one with spirit, with goodness,
And with faith.

Leave your troubled mind behind
And all confusion at the door.
Unwind the cares that grip your soul
And loose the weight of hate and war.

Come on over to peace that knows no end,
To clarity of thought and a purifying wind
That insists the pains you know depart
And heals the holes within your heart.

Concerns

Father/God/Mother/Sister/Brother/Friend would
you please help me with a few issues?

You know all things in and out of time,
in and out of me and all that is yet to be.
I worry, have concern about my future,
and of the many things I've yet to learn.

Then we'd recommend you come on home.

Home?

*It's the only way we can guarantee you'll be past the
steps of learning that await you. If you stay earth
bound expect upheaval of many kinds, noises in the
heavens, sorrow in your heart.*

Rats!

*But expect too, love, laughter, joy, a relinquishing
of struggling. Expect an emphasis of 'being', and of
being a blessing.*

Always Melchizedek you give me strength.
Tears may flow, but love is boundless.
You awaken me to hope; you cover me with grace; I
am settled in integrity. Thank you.

Corral Anger

Anger is a wild bull snorting fiercely.
With stomping hoofs he tosses his will about,
Or tosses his 'won't'!

Anger has a selfish side, it wants
its way again today.
It disputes challenges or reigning in.

Don't wish upon yourself the fate of that bull
Who is corralled, hobbled, chained
Until he learns manners or claims demise.

Instead dwell in kindness, in peace.
Desire not your own way,
Desire what is best for all, always.

Delight

Delight in honesty
Kindness
Truth
The energy of love
Compassion
A gentle wish
The light in a friend's eyes
and
your name whispered softly in the dark.

Doers

We 'do' and 'do' again, are busy day by day.
We don't stop helping - this is a role we play.

We work with happy song, smile with spirit light.
There's much to do, and we will do it right.

Let's also take time to simply 'be'.
Release from within the hidden 'me'.

Drenched

A storm of goodness has entrapped me.
I am drenched in abundance,
In monstrous opportunities,
And in love that knows no end.

From within and without
Spirit bubbles up
In joy and gladness
Washing away despair
And any sadness.

Drug of Choice

What is cold but absence of heat?
Or hate but lack of love?
What is anguish but lack of hope?
Fear, lack of understanding?

Fill the gap with energy -
The energies that 'be'.
They'll make us whole.
Goodness of Spirit sets one free.

Let compassion be our 'drug of choice'.
Extend a hand to each.
We will be filled, will overflow
With joy, wisdom, peace.

Let's be cautious of where we spend our cash,
Of where we place affection.
Be wise.
Dividends are not found in all transactions.

Earth Cries Out

The Earth, herself, cries out:

"I bleed, I ache;
I find it hard to breathe, to cope.
My surface is cluttered with decaying corpses,
the blood of many clogs the sands;
it seeps into rivers,
displacing the clarity needed for living.

Stop. Assess. Make improvements in thoughts
and actions or pay the consequences.

There are those, we know, who
hunger after righteousness,
but they are being dragged into
'the lowest common denominator'
as justice rains upon the evil
and the good are smitten too.

Wild animals will find your fallen bodies.
They will drink your blood, devour
your decaying flesh.

Unless you find a better way, there
will be no grave, no tomb.

Embrace Change

Embrace change.
Let Spirit abide fully.
Honor the past.
Delight in the present.

Expect the future to bring excitement,
the unfolding of Kindness,
Light,
Wisdom,
Peace,
Love.
And of these, love is the greatest.

Everlasting

'From everlasting to everlasting…'
what is that, I ponder.
I see naught that qualifies as 'Everlasting'.

All that is, and is to come, changes, grows,
becomes authentic, is renewed then finds itself
as dust or mold or ashes cast into the sea.

What seems to be 'set in stone' crumbles,
turns to dust, becomes the minerals which may,
one day, be within the plant devoured by me.

And thus, in some strange way, these molecules
follow my body into the grave but I'm not there.
Can you not see my spirit soar?

Then, with only a whispered good-bye,
and even as the body rots,
my spirit once again finds new places to explore.

Not dead, no end.
And that's as close to 'everlasting'
as this mind can comprehend.

Faithlessness

The faithlessness of another
Has hurt you to the core.
The attitude, the talk (so rude)
Surfaced from the depths one more.

Tears coursed down your cheeks
But you stood calm, tall and resolute.
You knew your life held pain
But also hope.

You've been through the fire before.
And you'll come through once more.

Await the peace you'll find in store.

Family

We're family; we're family right to the core.
We're one and the same whether we be
father or mother,
sister or brother,
cousin, friend,
stranger or neighbour.
We're family, family right to the core.

Praise to the father, the mother, the son,
Praise spirit within us all.
We're one of a crowd, let's say it once more,
We're family – right to the core.
Yes. We are family right to the core.

*Here's the hard working generation
that gave us birth.*

Feathers from the Wings of Our God

Let the touch of the feathers
Which fall from the wings of our God
Bring peace and make us whole.

May that touch refresh,
Clear our mind, give strength,
And reach our soul.

May the love held within
The touch of those feathers
Restore us to joy and gentleness.

May the God that we know
Reach our heart once more
Bringing health and healing through and through.

Spirit, you use whom you can.
You use who you do.

*I wrote this inspired poem some time ago; had occasion to
give a copy to Fiona whom I met at a retreat in Sedona; she
had come in from a walk with a short fluffy feather firmly
embedded in the hair behind her ear.*

*When I came across the poem recently I whispered to Spirit that
I would love a token like that myself. Lo and behold if I didn't
find one beside my bed this morning. I know it came from a
feather boa that I wore in a parade some years ago which has
since hung in my closet for years. Yet even knowing that, I feel
loved, refreshed.*

Forgiven

We have lived by our own devices.
We have cheated.
We have lied.
We've withheld blessings.
Our 'sins' we've tried to hide.

Yet, we are loved
And graciously accepted.
We live within a state of forgiveness.
Do we know this?
Do we claim this gift to us?

God, whoever you may be,
I feel your love,
Accept forgiveness freely given.
I ask you place your Spirit within.

With thanks, I say 'Amen'

Forgiveness?

Who are we
To withhold forgiveness from anyone?

Have we walked in their shoes?
Lived their life – hard won?

Do we recognize the path they walk is their
perfect path and the way that they must go?
We know not.

Let us therefore be generous with love,
And keep no hint of unforgiveness
from request.

Even as our higher power
never withholds from us opportunity to grow
but guides us in the way that we should go.

We are understood.
But we must make amends, and do good,
for *as we do, so shall it be done to us.*

Yep, it's still the old adage: *Do unto others
as you would have others do unto you.*
Or,
What goes around comes around,
Or,
Reap what you sow.

Fresh Start

I can get to Thursday – to Thursday,
'Cause Wednesday's come and gone.

I can get through Thursday
As Wednesday wasn't long.

I'll get past Friday
See the weekend come around.

I'll find in Saturday and Sunday,
The promise of a new week, and a new way,
With a song.

By Monday I'll have energy and plans
Tuesday - hope within and peace.

As the weeks roll on I'll find a fresh start;
A fresh start and everything I need.

Amen

Fret Not

There are perilous times ahead:
Upheaval
Shaking
Change of direction.

There are also times of joy
Delight
Discovery
Examination
And spiritual enlightenment.

Do not be afraid.
You do not die.
You are spirit, life itself. You cannot die.
They lie who tell you otherwise.

Though the body that houses
self may become worn
Crushed
or fragmented,
You are whole.
Perfect.
Everlasting.
Immutable.
Strong.

Words from One You Know

Relax, fret not, I am here in peace to set your feet upon a solid rock.

My solid rock? That's a good start. I pull across the carpet a heavy stone that rests within this space. I felt all morning that I should place my feet upon its cool surface – but procrastinated.

Alright. You are here now and of good intent.

Expect energy to descend upon you, to wake you up at night, to be in your daytime comings and goings. Smile as you go about your day to those nearby. Speak encouraging words from a centre of authority. What you say I hear. What you say, I'll do.

Oh, Lord, keep then a watch on my mouth, my heart, my intent. 'Twig' me when I go amiss.

I speak peace to North America – to those of us in Canada who have things 'good' or do not, I speak peace and prosperity.

To sons who have landed in jail – be released. Venture home, be reunited with loved ones – yes they love you yet. Be healed, seek Spirit.

To those who seek to harm, I say, hold back the intent. Do good instead.

I speak to darkness everywhere – give way to light. There is enough for everyone, there is a way, there is yet time to live, to work, to play.

To those who lie abed and want to rise – be risen!
To those who wish to leave – this is a given.
To those who choose to stay and receive the care they get, stay – be there yet.

To those who have no food to feed their young – receive manna from above. Hunger not.
You did it before my God, I know you can do it again....Mm, I hear what you are saying, we have to ask, so we know whom to thank – good advice.
Much obliged. We'll keep that in mind.

And before I go, I say - false system be gone, let a righteous way be ours, there is plenty - let it be shared. Amen

Gaia

Earth, our home, is not just rock and dust,
but is an entity, a being, Gaia.
She cries out now from pain within and pain without.
Her soul abused, skin rent, covered with scabs,
the waters in her veins putrefied,
and her atmosphere assaulted
has left her ill, sick unto death.

She twists, turns, vomits, cries in despair.
Her moaning is ignored;
her anguish falls on ears that will not hear.
Ill, not able to resist,
she's raped, plundered, left for dead.

How can we bring her back to vitality, to health?
We love her, desire her continued presence with us.

Love is a good beginning, tell her so.
Show her reasons to feel she's wanted, needed.
Clean and bandage her wounds,
Feed her no more filth.
Heed her heartfelt messages.
Give, expecting nothing in return.
Be gentle and subdued.
Want less, provide more.

So be it.
Gaia, Gaia, Gaia, our beautiful planet,
We love you and we'll make amends.
I'd like to say that's from all of us here on Earth;
Maybe it's not just yet, but we're a start.

Maureen and her spirit friends

God's Energy Surrounds Me

The energy of God surrounds me.
The hope of the almighty crowns me.

The steadfastness of the three-in-one,
The All-in-all pursues me,
Keeps me, enlightens,
Preserves, exonerates.

I will flourish – a balm to the needy
The downhearted or the despondent.

I am an elixir to those who hope,
Who pray, consider, allow, embrace.
I will be of good cheer, for I am at peace.

I will encourage and be encouraged.
Come join me as we see this day
fruit of our intentions.

Grace

There for the taking – grace;
a gift given though not deserved.
Given in abundance just for this – the taking!

Reach out, see self cleansed made whole,
indeed made holy.
We are precious beings going through
lessons with which we teach,
or in lessons in which we learn.

Grace keeps us steady, focused,
in line with what is righteous and kind.
Love and kindness outweigh righteousness.
Open self to love and kindness
see how righteousness is freely added.

Growth

We are here on planet earth to
grow, to learn, to see.
Here to enchant, to support, question, agree.
Here we become aware of new vistas,
While other dimensions become aware of us.

The planet rotates, skirts disasters,
Passes through its phases and revolutions,
For a time, as time is meted at this end,
Earth is home, teacher, doctor, friend.

While Earth endures, I too, endure.
I become stronger, clearly focused, substantial,
compassionate, caring, knowing, wise.
I spell out the place where I'll abide.

Grumpy?

Today, as always, we are offered a fresh start.

If we so desire, we can 'grump along', that is our choice.

Or, if we prefer, the day can be spent with smiles and a song.

Choice is ever present. Peace is ever possible.

Kindness for all is the 'icing on the cake'!

And whole hearted laughter might just get us on track.

Hallelujah!

Spirit's here, as ever,
Welcoming,
Forgiving,
Embracing me with love.

The times I've gone astray,
Not listened to God's voice,
Done wrong, or spoke amiss
Are swallowed by the righteousness of Christ.
And I?
I am loved, exonerated, held close,
Swaddled in the Light.

....

Step up, step forward,
Step gently with a whisper,
Or roar loud and clear for all to hear:

There is righteousness at hand,
There are debts which are forgiven,
Sloppy speech which is erased.

There's a planting of goodness in its place.
Come,
See a mushrooming of gentleness and grace.

Hallelujah!

Harm Not nor Hinder Growth

Who are you to harm another?

Would you have what you exhibit, come back with force upon you?

'What goes around comes around', is a popular saying. It is also a law on the planet – you've witnessed this time and time again.

Therefore, harm not. And hinder not the learning and the growth of another.

Have a Good Day

Have a good day.
Yes, have a good day!
As your days, so your life.

A 'good day' does not consist only of rest,
refreshment, pleasant times.

In a good day we may experience a struggle
which makes us seek understanding,
Or pain, which leads to temperance.

It may be words which stop, give thought,
Allow one to ponder direction.

The 'good' in good day comes from knowing -
Knowing there is a universal plan for life,
There is strength to see us through our journey;

there is love from within and without.
And there is an abundance of joy
Which springs forth just from being.

Have a great day!

Higher Ground, Please

Lift me up, Lord, lift me higher
So that I'm where I should be.
Let me be on higher ground,
Higher ground where peace is found.

Let me share Lord that higher place
Share it now with love and grace.
Help us all find that higher ground
Higher ground where peace abounds.

May we all live on higher ground, Lord,
Imbued with wisdom freely given.
Let us act like we belong
Here at home on higher ground.

Lift me up, Lord, lift me higher
So that I'm where I should be.
Let me be on higher ground,
Higher ground where peace is found.
Amen

Heed

Avoid the sound of angry words,
Seek peace.
Look for the quiet corner.

Allow Spirit to descend before you say a word.
Maintain equilibrium.
Smile. Nod. Listen.

Pay attention to what is 'said' beneath
what is being said.
Care deeply.
Attend well.

Hope is the Seed of Reality

Hope is the seed of reality.
Plant it. Water it.
Let sunshine give it warmth;
Breezes refresh.

Day by day see reality grow.
Feel the excitement of life taking root,
Of gladness reaching heavenward,
Of the fruit of expectation come to be.

Reward is reality
Which has been carefully nurtured.
Which was there before the seeds were
planted, or broke through the soil.

And here it is again-
The reality you need
found hiding in the hope you planted
yesterday in faith.

How Wonderful the Strands of Heaven

How wonderful to take the strands of heaven

The strings of nature's plan

And weave a grid around the earth

Empowering it, and all within.

How wonderful to heal intentions,

Lift our spirits, change our mind,

Help us find pure love, peace,

And wisdom of a godly kind.

How wonderful we all can see,

As God always has,

Mankind – righteous, filled with hope,

Walking perfect paths.

I Know God Loves Me

How wonderful to know God loves me.
How wonderful to know He's real.
How wonderful to know she'll never leave me
Takes my hand and ever leads me
How wonderful,
How wonderful,
How wonderful indeed.

How wonderful to know God listens.
To know s/he's always by my side,
Leads me on the path that I should go.
And one day s/he will take me home.
How wonderful,
How wonderful,
How wonderful that's known.

How wonderful to know God holds us
And carries half the load.
How wonderful He lifts our burdens
And gives us peace untold.
How wonderful,
How wonderful,
How wonderful for all who know.

God loves you, too, and always will
No matter what you've done or do.
Ask for forgiveness, determine to do better,
Learn. Let Jesus visit you.
How wonderful.

How wonderful to know God's love is true.

I Sing

When I consider this amazing globe,
I sing!
Joy fills my heart
A song is on my lips.
My heart soars.

Thank you Father for our planet,
For family and friends.

Thank you for the spirit within
That never ends
But lives to play once more
Or enters All-in-All
As part of all that is.

If It's Good for Me?

If it's good for me, could it be good for you?

Recently Spirit gave me some advice. I know my 'good' was Spirit's intention so have been trying to follow through with the ideas. I include this advice here thinking 'If it's good for me, maybe you, my friends, will benefit too.'

Message to Maureen

Many would give their 'eye-teeth', so to speak, to be in your shoes. You have friends, freedom, time, support, togetherness. That's 'all good'. You have time to work, to play, and opportunities for activities, visiting, writing, uplifting. You are in a win-win situation - blessed. Keep it up.

Here's a hint for health: eat less dairy, more greens. Lift your eyes to heaven, your heart to the stars. Welcome change. Laugh at (seeming) setbacks. Walk forward with no fear just great anticipation.

I'm a Being "Being"

'Who are you?' and...
'Who do you think you are?' I was asked.

Me? Hmmm... I'm a 'has been'.
I'm a 'has been' cause I've been
A being many a time.
I was being a 'being' in all of those past lives.

And I'm a 'being' being.
Yes, here I am.
In the now I am being -
A being being a 'being' once again.

And I'm a 'wanna be',
For I'll be being once more
When you think I'm dead and gone.
I'll be being within the All-in-All,
I'll be being part of the One.

*I'm aware of many lives I've had in the past;
obviously when I died I wasn't really dead – just
off on a new adventure. I'm convinced there is
no death, so.... meet you on the other side!*

Till then, Blessings! Maureen

In Christ, Liberty

We have been encompassed
In the shell we know as body
But one day it will crack and set us free.
Ahh, in Christ's understanding, liberty.

There's a struggle to expect - that's for sure
For it's not easy getting out of here.
And that seems to be the status quo
whether we are being born
or abandoning the life we know.

We leave the comfort of this plane,
Face the joys and pain of who we've been,
See lessons learned and experiences perceived.
They enlarged the person that we now 'be'.

Death is not an ending I'm convinced
but a release of energy,
An opportunity for new beginnings, new possibilities.
There are things yet to discover
I missed doing them this trip.
'Practice love' is what I recommend
to those who follow in my steps.

Recently God told me that when I die I do not need to come back to another lifetime if that is my choice. (I've been through a lot of those.) If I am ready I can join Source and be at one with the All-in-All. I have been giving this some thought and think that I am ready. It is not an easy choice to make as I'm so used to having a body, but I'm also used to being spirit within, so..... I know I can do it... though I'm not in a rush. Wish me well! Wish us all well!

Is It a Kindness?

Is it a kindness to always speak kindly?
Is it honest to hide hard truths?
Does one fulfill her part ignoring,
hiding, overlooking?

Is it right to 'tell it like it is?'
Is it wrong to grant white lies?

Does one complete one's task
accepting irresponsibility?

*There must be balance, moderation
and love in all things.*

In Goodness, Trust

Create goodness within; see it multiply and spill out to touch many.

See goodness bring about the fruit of goodwill and godliness. See it steep within and flow without. And as it flows it carries many in its energy.

See, in goodness, lives transformed, relationships healed, the poor in spirit made whole.

And when you do see these things come to pass, give thanks.

Abide in unity.
Trust fellowship and friendship to do their 'magic'.

Is This What We Leave?

Who litters and pollutes the nest?
Idiots, mindless masters.

Who craps in their own bed?
The insane, the dying, the mislead.

Who ignores another's poverty and pain?
The heartless, the greedy, the inhumane.

Who pays no mind to our planet's harm?

This is what we leave?
This what we choose for our children?
This the inheritance our grandchildren receive?

Cleanse the sea. Refresh the air.
Change protocol.

Let rivers, streams, love and new intent
Bring wholeness to our globe, our soul

And life and living to us all.

Amen

It's Not All about Us

Life is about the whole, the community,
creation and the evolution of humankind.

It is not all about 'us' individually,
even though we may be the 'book' that is read.

Let us start with finesse,
Live in magnificence,
End with glory.

And through it all may the being which we are
be filled with love and living.

Give, and in giving receive;
that which you need and deserve will appear.
Bless, be a blessing,
Be blessed.

Jesus Is My Brother

He fed the hungry, healed the broken,
Touched hearts, claimed, forgave and pardoned.
That was Jesus...
And Jesus is my brother.

God's within, as we now know; we too are gifted.
The lame will walk, burdens shall be lifted.
That's me... and thee.
For Jesus is our brother.

We'll do as He - encourage spirits, cleanse
intention, Raise the dead, provide direction.
That's you and me,
because Jesus is our brother.

I had a hard time with some of this – particularly the 'Raise the dead' statement. However God showed me that every day doctors, police officers, rescue personnel and concerned citizens snatch souls from certain death. I was humbled as I was included due to my intervention in two incidences when I called 911, then kept thoughtful watch over the subjects until ambulances and paramedics arrived. M

Just as You Are

You are loved, additionally, you are
accepted, just as you are.
In days to come you'll make changes in
thoughts and actions, but that's for tomorrow.

Today you are loved 'as is'.
Know you are blessed for the sake of the 'blessing',
Not for anything you've done or accomplished.
Wear this 'knowing' inside and out.

Join Me as I Cry

Tears whelm my eyes
Course down my cheeks
Leave soggy stains upon my book.
I hurt because I care.
I hurt because I share your burdens.

As handmaiden of Spirit,
Compassionate, caring, thoughtful,
I am gentle, yet strong -
In touch with the light that floods us all.

Join me as I cry.
Together let our tears appear.
Be not mindful of the pain,
But see the others side of things.

See realms from whence we came
And 'home' to where we soon return.
See loved ones join in happiness.
Hearts aglow with love, acceptance.

Life isn't always easy
But life is what we choose.
Be good to self. Be kind to all.
Love. Hope, when all else fails.

Let's Aim for Kindness

Let's aim for kindness,
A kindness which receiver would find a blessing,
Not one that suits us best.
Not one of our making.

Kindness is not always found
within the golden rule:
Do unto others as you'd have them do to you.
No. Kindness is doing unto
others what *they* desire.
For they may be ahead, or lag behind somewhere.
But there they are, though you are here,
Accept what there you find.

This is not to say that you become
the image of that soul. No. Hold your
own. It has likely taken 'lifetimes'
for us to be the one that people see.
Another's path is for just them,
not what we need to be.

All 'truth' need not be shared or said, nor spared.
Be good, be kind. Be honest with a twist.
Where does Spirit lead? What can friend accept?
What does Jesus say through my lips?

Help the hurting, encourage the disappointed,
wrap your arms around the bereaved.

Loose Attachment

The path of life has twists and turns.
It's rough and tangled; often
Overgrown with pain, disease, discouragement.
Other times it's clearly defined.

Loose attachment to destination.
Instead - capture essence of the journey.
Delight in the day, the weather,
The companion who walks by your side.

Be buoyant of spirit.
Let light shine through your eyes
Let healing harbour in your touch.
All is well, as it ought to be.

Listen. Heed.

This entity is before you Spirit, with thanksgiving and health, feeling there is something she needs to know.

(Perchance you need to know this too.)

Today, you are blessed and a blessing. Be of good cheer. All is well in your heart, your soul, your mind. Continue to bless others, and to let others bless you.

Live in God's Wisdom

Let's open our hearts
as the space where we listen.
Let's give thanks as we live in God's wisdom.
We'll be grateful, expectant – not frozen in time,
For we are connected to the divine.

We are beloved, part of an expanding family.
We will be of good cheer –
for all we need is given, amply.

We have the light, health,
finances and joy we need.
Our strength and loving outlook are guaranteed.
Thank you Spirit; yes, thank you indeed.

Listeners

We hear a voice carried in the wind,
the ache within a worried mind.
We know the hurt a spirit feels, its pain
When insults and put-downs are hurled.

Vibration of anxiety
is clear in temper and in tone;
This person needs a quiet space,
the comfort of a warm and tender home.

Another should be wrapped in peace,
held close by those who care and really listen.
Agitated taken for a walk and gentle talk,
cranky left alone, a sullen one forgiven.

Sometimes we hear joy bubble from the soul,
hugs abound, laughter fills the air,
How glad we are to know, that for today,
love is everywhere!

May we be the eyes that see, the ears which
hear, and may we find a way to make
things clear to our family and friends –
and to those we hold dear.

And let us not forget those who are new to
the wonders of God, the wisdom of Spirit,
the closeness of kindness, the strength
which is found in a friend.

Look Up, Look Ahead

Do not look from whence you came,
Nor to places where you've been.

Look up, look ahead,
Look in love at what you see.

Protect the one who needs it,
The lazy steward - provoke.

Belie the wicked speech
You know is wrong.

Get in the boat with others
Who proclaim that God within knows best.

Paddle with enthusiasm
While your spirit is at rest.

Look up, see peace descend,
Hear echoes of abundance frame the land.

Know all are on the path
They have chosen for themselves, as are you.

Grasp the 'big picture'
Which escapes mortal time.

See instead the perfect pathways
Of footprints in the sand.

Look Up, See Heaven Open

Look up, see heaven open
See angels, family friends.
See the outstretched arms of loved ones
Welcoming you to life that never ends.

They have been with you a while
(They checked in from time to time)
Though you thought that they were gone
They often hovered at your side.

Embrace, shed tears of joy, catch up, laugh,
play, enjoy continuum of passage.
Regroup; be ready for another time
When you will once again
Set forth on an adventure of body, soul and mind.

Lord, I Feel Your Anointing
What Sayest Thou?

You are right to pay attention for I have much to tell you, sayeth your God.

Know you are in the right space. All is well in your own life, and is as it should be,

> *For this I thank you, my*
> *Father/Mother/ Sister/Brother/ Cousin/Friend.*

There are many who suffer not only the pangs of physical hunger as this world unwinds, but there are many who hunger for hope. They need to see in real time that they are loved and accepted and that there is a place for them, too, in 'heaven' as you call it.

> *What shall I tell them?*

Today you find yourself in in a solid state, three dimensional as it were. Tomorrow you may find yourself instead as a frame without substance but with light and understanding. In either form you are loved and heard and in a place where you can be blessed and a blessing.

Lord Thou Art Altogether
High, Mighty, Lifted Up

Thou art altogether high, mighty, lifted up
And yet, lord, close at hand;
As close as our turning to you
to be wrapped in your gentleness,
kindness, and rest.

Help us to hear while we can yet hear.
Help us to hear while your voice
is not overwhelmed
by noises of the atmosphere or
the confusion in our lives.

Help us to hear while we can hear.

Set our minds to be receptive, our
ears tuned to the right station,
The station of love and goodness.

Love is One Part Blindness

Love is one part blindness
of another's shortcomings.

It's two parts kindness,
With more kindness held in store

Add three parts acceptance
And surely you will find

That love is amply rewarded
By the joy you hold within.

Love Is Such an Amazing Thing

Love is such an amazing thing.
There's no end to this commodity.
No need to portion it out in little bits.
No need to be miserly.

The loss of one you love
May seem to break your heart.
But if that love was taken, or trod upon, or spurned
It may not be your fault.

Love is a wonderful thing
It defies the theory of economics.
It is not valued more because of short supply.
No need to ration it or hide it in a vault.

Sometimes love hurts, that's true.
And loving is a risk for others and for you.

Know this - you'll find love yet
From whence love makes its way.
And when it does, let it flood your soul.
Let love pass through you to those who need it too.

If you only have a little,
You still have got a lot.
With the little you have, and the more you give,
The more you'll have to share.

The more you share, the more returned.
And more for everyone is there.
You'll be surprised how it multiplies
How it bubbles from your heart.

You'll be drenched, and steeped in love.
And life will be good once more.

Love Is....What?

When I heard the expression below the other day,
I must admit it made me give my head a shake!

'Love is never having to say you're sorry'?

What's this?
I've heard that expression, but, pardon me,
it just might not work for some of us.

Yes, as long as we dwell in love 24 hours a day, we
likely won't have an opportunity to say we're sorry.

On the other hand, sometimes we may
step out of the 'love zone' and do or say
something we ought not to do or say.

Yet that doesn't mean I don't love you anymore.
Upon reflection we know we were out of line.
Does this ever happen to you, too?

Then 'Sorry' is certainly in order.
And so is 'God keep me mindful of
staying, always, in the realm of 'love'.
May we, indeed, be given the grace
and strength to keep us there.

Love - the Original Renewable Resource

Love is the original renewable resource.
Plant it in a corner of your soul,
Within your mind,
And in the things you do and know.

Water it with grace and hope,
Feed it faithfully.
Watch it sprout, grow roots
Get stronger day by day.

See the light and joy it brings;
Reap, and reap again;
Spread it generously -
There's more from where that came.

Spread it in the neighborhood,
Deliver abundantly.
Give to all, withhold from none
Love is granted graciously.

Lovely Altogether

The Lord is wise, lovely altogether.
Yes, the Lord is wise and lovely altogether.
His feet shine like polished gold.
Her eyes are coals of fire.
The Lord is lovely all together.

His hands are gentle; they reach out to me and you.
Her voice is soft and kind, our voice is soft and kind.
Listen to this voice, for this voice is kind and soft.
It speaks to the heart within.

The Lord, the Lord has shoulders broad
Broad shoulders to help us carry our load,
God carries our burdens, does it with a smile.
If we let our burdens rest, they'll be carried.

The Lord's chin is strong. His chin is strong.
For she's resolute, adamant, and
love shines through.
The Lord, the Lord is beautiful, thoughtful, kind.
Let this kind of beauty shine through you.

Just as the Father holds the Son, so Spirit holds us,
And holds us near for we are one.
We'll not be let go though we walk away,
Not if we walk away.
She'll not let go, even if we run.

Turn around. Turn and listen... seek Spirit's face.
Let grace be yours, let wisdom enfold you.
Turn around to a welcome and a warm embrace,
Let Spirit
now enfold you.

Feeling Manipulated?

Sometimes, me thinks,

There is collusion between 'the market'
and 'the press'.

For every time one 'loses'
Another 'wins'
Would be my guess.

And who knows
what franchised news can do?
Could it benefit, perchance,
those who write this mess?

With odds not stacked for folk like me
I skip 'the market',
Put frugality and virtue to the test.
For me ....that works best.

Missing a Loved One

I see the doors of heaven open
The gentle light explores
The crowd who've come to meet me.
And in among them – there you are!

You've been waiting for awhile.
You've often watched this gate.
Now, here I am.
Right on time, not late.

I've had business to attend to,
Words to write, hurts to mend,
As I, too, have waited for this day.
Now here I am, my friend.

Please take my hand and lead me in.
There's lots to catch up on -
We have timelessness for that,
and timelessness for fun!

My Cup Overflows

We are blessed with abundance,

A cup that overflows,

A life which nurtures us

And those around.

Ever are we loved.

Always do we love.

So it is,

And so it shall continue

Till time departs,

The sky is rolled away

And alone

I stand before my God.

My God is Love

My God is not gender specific
Nor does s/he sit upon a throne.
Does not make pronouncements
Or harshly judge.

My God is love, kindness, wisdom.
Energy in motion,
The all-in-all vibration who waits always.
Never despairs.

Who sees for each gladness, growth,
Freshness of Spirit
And a satisfying, expected end.
Not an end as ending...

But an end which leads to new beginning,
Where, on unique path, we continue,
Or take flight in dimensions
Yet to be known.

"My Life is My Own"

Do you have the right to say
"My life is my own"?
Are you not the child of sperm from your father's
loins given refuge in your mother's womb?

Are you not the hope and dreams that
brought about your entry here on earth?
Sleepless nights, tossing to and fro,
nausea, anxiety:
All these and more are placed upon the
threshold of the door that gives you birth.

Your life is wrapped in pleasure, pain,
delight, ignorance, joy and wonder.
And though we fail at times, it is our want to lead
you on a path that makes you strong, forthright,
kind, conscious of the will of self and others.

Hold fast to what is good,
to what is right and true.
Forgive, we pray, our shortcomings;
Accept guidance from within
and from the 'powers that be'.
You walk on hallowed ground.
Your life is part of today and of eternity.

No Reflection on You

Forget hurts of the past,
slights, rough talk, thoughtless action,
or inaction,
rude gestures, ignorant comments,
shouted threats, abuse.
These reflect not on who you be,
but, rather, are indication of the learning
still ahead for those who so do.

You are kind, thoughtful, of good intent.

You are spirit in guise of human form.

Remember who you are.

Not Good Enough

There are times, I know,
When 'my best' has not been good enough.
Somehow I've let you down
I have failed at the task I set myself.

I have not been gentle, or softly spoken.
Have been a little 'testy', abrupt, demanding.
If you are one that feels this way,
Please, may I be forgiven?

God has not given up on me.
I'm trying to follow that example.
My intention is to not give up on self.
With grace and kindness I'll do better.

And if you feel the same,
(which is possible at this time)
Let's make a pact with a high five
And move towards love again.
Amen

Once Was I?

Once was I a wisp of smoke? Once was I a queen?
Did I know without a word, telepathically?
Was I the dolphin frolicking in the sea with
a dolphin lover who took good care of me?

Did I walk on beaches which
now the sea has covered?
Levitate? Understand planetary struggles?

Have I been in Egypt, danced within Stonehenge?
Or emigrated from Pleiades
with intent to seed this sphere?

Was I the youth, pretty lass, who
took up with a pirate?
Was I burnt at the stake, by those
who knew not truth?

Did I leave beloved England with
hope and with my son?
Looking for a home, a new land to call my own?

Punished for my faith, was I shot, dumped
into pit, and suffocated there?

And now that I am here, knowing there's
no death, none to fear, can I be light,
a beacon to the wondering ones?

Can I steer the curious, the thoughtful, to live from their heart? And will I do what I've been taught: love, demanding naught?

Will I encourage acceptance of each soul where that soul is at? Will I do the same? Perceive growth and learning, laying down no blame?

I would, even though this path might tax my body and inflame my mind, my soul will rest in peace when I transition from this shell.

I'll return to Source, to God, to
Christ, to Emmanuel.
And with the many that do
likewise there we'll dwell.

One Great System

I saw wake behind the boat
Send waves onto the shore.

Saw the waves interrupt, so briefly,
The ebbing of the tide.

Watched in wonder as water washed over cliffs
Into earth's welcoming.

It did what it must do, and
Before it moved along, parched land revived.

Then the molecules of water joined with others,
Settling calmly as a dew.

That adventure completed
Once again were lifted high.

Next they clung with watery friends
In storm magnificent.

We were spell bound, held in awe
As bits of water turned to snow and ice.

Each watery molecule, part of one great
system, knows not edge or boundary;

Nor does Spirit. Together we are one.
As majestic as is water, so too, may we be found.

Outside the Lines

Set before me, today, is opportunity
with no lines to guide me.
Today, where I will, I walk, talk, frown, smile.
I'm free to be me for awhile.

Spirit of God; help me be, I pray, generous, kind,
Encouraging, honest in a thoughtful way.
Let me be grandma, and a loving mother,
Sister, cousin, stalwart friend, and neighbour.

New Suit for the Deck of Cards

Ah, a new suit for the deck of cards...
...the star... Spirit indeed!

Light to shine in dark places.

Hope to brighten the sky.

Radiant glory to enliven our spirit.

Energy to cast its healing spell.

The star trumps all,

Brings to naught spade, club,
diamond, even heart.

Its glory leads us on to greater feats.

Courage, kindness, wisdom

Are encompassed in its light.

Its rays awaken strength, learning, generosity.

They act as magnet to the pure, the kind,

Those of integrity.

The clan thus drawn shall pave the way

And we shall see tomorrow's peace with us today.

No Reflection on You

Forget hurts of the past,
slights, rough talk, thoughtless action,
or inaction,
rude gestures, ignorant comments,
shouted threats, abuse.
These reflect not on who you be,
but, rather, are indication of the learning
still ahead for those who so do.

You are kind, thoughtful, of good intent.

You are spirit in guise of human form.

Remember who you are.

What's this: Love is Never Having to Say you're Sorry?

Right! You won't have to ever say you're sorry
as long as you dwell in love 24 hours a day –
every day.

However, sometimes we step out of the love zone
and do or say something we ought not do or say.

Upon reflection we know we were out of
line. Then *"Sorry"* is certainly in order.

And so is
*"God, keep me mindful of staying,
always, in the love zone."*

May we, indeed, be given grace and
strength to speak with love.

On a need to know basis...

What Do I Need to Know About Forgiveness?

What is there that needs forgiveness?
There is naught.
You were, and are, whole-heartedly
walking your perfect path;
as are those who enter into your own life.

See self reflected in the mirror of others.
If you see something that annoys you, it is that
which you must eliminate in your own life.

Do not seek to forgive or to be forgiven.
Seek instead magnanimity in love.

Overlook another's fault.

Pay Attention

Drop everything – pay attention.
No harm will come to you.
You are learning what is important
And what is 'Tommy-rot'.

You are learning what deserves attention
And what does not,
What is worth pursuing?
And what is that which should be forgotten.

Continue paying attention.

Praise Whelms

Hallelujah, Hallelujah, Hallelujah.

Praise whelms within my heart.

The joy I know,

The peace within,

Are treasures which will never end.

The pain – I leave, the troubles, too.

I will not grasp their ilk again.

For you will find me in a lighted space

No spot, no wrinkle, turmoil gone.

And in their place a holiness.

Amen

Perfect Path

Our perfect path holds joy, tranquility,
And likely pain and sorrow.
For as we live and learn and love
We advance, retreat, and stretch to grow.

Sometimes the winding of the path
Is about us and the way that we must turn.
At other times it's for another.
And dimensions she must learn.

Sometimes in glee, with great abandon,
We roll down the hill.
At other times we struggle in the darkness
But must trudge on still.

Ups and downs are to be expected
For we stumble, fall or part.
Here we need a friend to patch our 'owies',
Help us mend our aching heart.

And he will lift your spirit
And she will grant you peace
And you will find that in the moment
Love and wisdom are released.

So take not the path of least resistance
But the way that you must go.
On our perfect path we're given grace
Which will see us through.

Prayer at Night-time

Now I lay me down to sleep
I pray oh God, my soul you'll keep.

If I should die before I wake,
I pray my soul you'll take.

I rest in you and in your grace.
Whether I leave or stay in this place.

One day, I know, I'm heaven bent,
Reunited with you, my spirit content.

You are, oh God, the eternal I Am.
You see me whole and forgiven.

I close my eyes, and rest my head;
I am at peace in you, settled here in bed.

We're so close we are one.
Knowing this I sleep. Amen and Amen

Put Life to the Test

Is there any point is writing this?
Would you heed it anyhow? Would I?

Any point in reading what you hesitate to trust?
What do you know about the
person who has written this?

Let the spirit that's within the words you find,
be shaken as are pebbles in a sieve.

Let the sand fall away, keep the nuggets.
Let them help you live a life that's fuller,
a life that will never be erased
nor leave you distressed.

Be not afraid of dying, there is no such thing
as 'death'. More to the point is this – do not
be afraid of living – put life to the test.

Feel the rain upon your face, grass between your
toes, the warmth of a hug, perfume of the rose.
Live and love with gusto, revel in each day
Today is for the living, may we live it that way.

Raindrops

Raindrops soon are river,
River feeds the plain,
Lakes grow, flowers flourish,
Beauty erupts again.

Then from the lake watery molecules fly
Heading for the trees, the sky,
Eternity and all that is.

Ah, glorious!
But soon they're back with us;
Waiting for another turn around their 'universe'.

Rattled

You feel 'rattled' today.
Leave it and come to peace.
Settle in to the heart of God,
or the Spirit that you know.
This is where you are loved, cherished,
and made whole.

Be one with the All-in-all. Relax.
Dream a dream that sees you in plenty,
in health and with abundant opportunities
for service, kindness, growth,

Your situation is as it is for a reason, for
a season, for your expansion and for a
life 'change' which will present itself.

Make some plans, write the notes,
see them come to pass.
Look back, I ask, and report to self
the lessons learned, the grace and growth.
Then smile and give thanks
and ponder your blessings awhile.

Renewal

A river flows past this home,
It waters all, quenches thirst,
Helps the grasses grow.

Fish dance within its gentle flow,
Dragonflies hover,
Gnats come and go.

All are welcome at the river's bank.
All may play, may swim,
May be refreshed, made whole.

Spirit is the river, the refreshing, the renewal.
Come, jump right in, splash about,
Intensify your soul.

Rest Assured

Rest assured that you will have
Strength for tomorrow's tasks,
Peace to meet any crisis,
Love to abundantly share,
Wisdom to fulfill obligations.

You'll have joy with which to meet the day,
Food upon your plate,
Gentle conversation in your mouth,
And a pillow upon which
You'll lay your head once more.

Righteousness – Gift from God

Righteousness is within our soul.
Soul inhabits heart, it's true
But also – every molecule.

Lean towards righteousness
And see it grow.

Given just a little prod in the right direction
Righteousness will be set in motion.

Temptations will dissolve and loose their hold.
Righteousness can then unfold.

So... let's determine now to listen
to the righteousness within.

This gift will keep us pure again, and again.

Servers

Whatever we do we represent our self;
As well, we may represent an employer.
Of course we represent, too, all of humanity.
This is no small thing!

Let us do what we do respectfully, with
positive openness and cheerful disposition.
See all work as beneficial, done graciously,
considering those who will benefit
from our actions.

We'll lay our head upon our pillow,
after a day well spent,
in peace, with gladness of heart,
we'll sleep knowing we will be refreshed
inwardly and strengthened in body and mind.

Small Miracles

Walking through a local mall yesterday,
a small buoyant object caught my eye.
I stooped and picked it up,
Ah, a small feather, down like.

How could that possibly have got in here?
....

When I spot a feather in an unusual place
it's like a reminder of God's love and grace.

Thank you Father for being near, for being
mindful of me. Thank you for this token.

I know you are close, never far away;
That my best interests are yours
Always and today.

Please use this reminder for my friends, too,
May they know at a feather's view
that they are loved by you.

And may they stop and visit awhile
then leave with happy heart and smile :)

Smile Supply

As I dip into my 'smile supply'
and find a few to share,
I'm surprised to find discernment, contentment,
And laughter, too, is there.

I've a lot to give;
I haven't run out yet
For I find the more I give
The more I'm bound to get.

I'm never stingy with the hugs, blessings,
Encouragement or a smile.
I start with love and kindness
For I know each one's worthwhile.

There's plenty for the folks just down
the street, and for my family, too.
Plenty for those near or far away
And of course there's enough for you!

Spirit Breathes Upon the Globe

Spirit breathes upon the globe; go with its flow.
Allow its momentum to be yours,
Its intention to soak your soul.

Listen, feel, hear, and know.

A mapping of a path for you appears:
Of knowledge, goodness, wisdom.
Simply 'be', relax, and have no fear.

Walk this path with joy and acceptance.
Have no hidden agenda.
Bless and be blessed in this moment and always.

Spell out the Place Where You'll Abide.

We are here on planet earth to
grow, to learn, to see.
Here to enchant, to support, question, agree.
Here we become aware of new vistas,
While other dimensions become aware of us.

The planet rotates, skirts disasters,
Passes through its phases and revolutions,
For a time, as time is meted at this end,
Earth is home, teacher, doctor, friend.

While Earth endures, I too, endure.
I become stronger, clearly focused, substantial,
compassionate, caring, knowing, wise.
I spell out the place where I'll abide.

Come, join me. Endure.
Become strong, clearly focused, substantial.
Embrace compassion, caring, knowledge, wisdom.
Spell out the place where you'll abide.

Spirit Searches

Always does Spirit search
For the soul which cares,
The heart that really listens,
The hands that govern righteously,
Love which intervenes.

Kindness, forgetfulness of transgressions,
Acceptance, grace, openness,
Delight, and thankfulness
Bring one to the brink of godliness,
Which is what Spirit seeks.

Come walk with me;
Let's offer our hands, our ears, our heart
Let love spill on all we see.
Let's be open, accountable, thankful'
Living righteously.

Spirit Seeks

Always does Spirit search
For the soul which cares,
The heart that really listens,
The hands that govern righteously,
Love which intervenes.

Kindness, forgetfulness of transgressions,
Acceptance, grace, openness,
Delight, and thankfulness
Bring one to the brink of godliness,
Which is what Spirit seeks.

Standing in Grace

I am but vibrations – vibrations of energy.
Some of this energy takes form,
Some is song, light, love, or misery.

I choose to stand within the space
Where I hear the tune, the words,
Feel utter acceptance which comes my way.

I am standing in a place
Where I can see, and hear and know.
Standing here in grace.

Beloved, embraced, encouraged, set free am I.
In spirit, and other degree of energy
I'm lifted up into the skies.

From these heights
I see a multitude of homes where I might live,
Where I might dwell and grow.

What seems to be the Earth,
What seems to be 'right now'
Is where I find myself.

So... here I make the best of things;
My feet touch the ground,
Yet my heart and soul take wings.

This is my niche for now;
Time to be alone, in conversation with a friend,
Or part of a busy crowd.
It's 'all good'. It's where I decide to be.
In this moment, in this place I give thanks;
My heart is open; my mind goes along for the ride.

Spring Erupts in Song

Green the grass and green the trees
As spring erupts in song.

'Green' the way to live our lives
All year long.

Exhibit kindness to the planet,
Kindness to each creature,

Oneness with the God we know
And with one another.

Be Still
Consider Truth and Knowledge

Truth: Let us exhibit truthfulness and honesty in our encounters and exchanges. Let correctness and accuracy colour our speech and writing.

Knowledge: There is a set of 'facts' which accompany many subjects and topics. There are also parameters of understanding and wisdom which we have accumulated over the centuries.

Upon this globe we find various cultures and the customs mores and folkways which contain ideas considered conducive to the welfare of society within these trends we get glimpses of truth and knowledge, but also colored interpretations.

However truth is true, and to be shared, and so are these 'knowings'. In that vein they are presented also. May the spirit of the God we know help us sift the dross from the pure.

Our Slate Wiped Clean

Today, if we so choose, our slate is wiped clean; the scars life has left in and upon these bodies are erased; we are refreshed within and without.
Yes, if we so choose, a new beginning is ours.
Memories, experiences, lessons learned are still here for us to use. The only thing gone is the list of 'wrongs' we thought were held against us.

Know this – that list has ever so been erased; each day has been and always will be a fresh start. Not to say this gives you 'carte blanche' to disobey the eternal laws which inhabit your heart. No. Look within and see what ought to be and help it come to be.

I hear these words, I look within.
I'll go forth in love with grace and kindness.

I thank you Spirit for going the distance with me.

Amen.

Rise Above Materialism

We live in a material world; as spiritual beings this is, presently, our 'training' ground. Those whose lives we touch live also in a material world – often without the truth and knowledge which Spirit provides. Within this frame work it is our job to provide opportunity for spiritual unraveling and growth for others even as we ourselves accept the same for self. We set the example be desiring the gracious energy of God lead us and use us, over the desire for material.

None of this is to say that material accoutrements negate the learning we desire; for it may be that having no concern for acquiring additional goods is due in part to knowing there is already, and always, food for our hunger, a bed for our head. However let us shake off the desire for 'more', for 'bigger, 'better', 'newer'. We will rise above materialism as we instead set goals of kindness, righteousness and acceptance.

Knock at the door of interest and inquisitiveness. There go with the flow into greater horizons. Lead but do not push. Understand. Do not demand understanding. Your light, your love, will reach into many dark corners and will brighten the lives of many.

113

A Word to Women

It has come to my attention that we are in a new world as women... we find professionals, politicians, and pragmatists in this category. We find mothers, grandmas, and women entering the world of 'work' or 'senior living' in this category.

Blessings to us as we bring a sense of fairness, gentleness, thoughtfulness to the world in which we find ourselves. Recognize this – we must be prepared to stand by the contracts we make, the agreements we sign.

Take into account however, that this transition may be difficult and hard to come to terms with not only by selves but by others – including all genders. Recognize your role in bringing about a peaceful transition through gentle and fair means.

And at this time consider that honesty and carefulness may be mottoes that we need to keep in mind. Support one another, do so in kindness. Be pragmatic and responsible. Look up and see God's gracious hand, but also look around; watch where you stand. May we be protected by fine men, by the law and by the God we love.

Adversity

Even in the face of adversity remain pure and holy. Take 'the hit' rather than succumb to wayward plans. Allow Spirit to weave for you a path and a way whereby you will harm none, nor be harmed.

When adversity leaves and once again clear wholesome days arrive, give thanks, give alms, give from the heart to the heart of another who is perhaps now meeting head on the with adversity that visited you.

Some say, "If it doesn't kill you it will make you stronger." Yes, you will become stronger and you will be a model for others. And in time you will give witness to the truth 'There is No Death'. But in the meantime go by faith and in the Spirit simply rest.

Be blessed and a blessing
Amen.

Build or Tear Down

Today a young man smiled and chattered cheerfully as he helped with bags of groceries. His pleasant disposition cheered me and healed us all.

The hairdresser untangled concerns and pain of her despondent client, while cutting, fashioning hair. In doing so she untangled pains of many.
Another soul dropped everything to lend a hand to fallen friend. We all were lifted.

The graciousness of thoughtful speech enlightened me. We all became much lighter. But when frustrated driver let go with a mouth of rage and gutter talk, we all were dissed.

Whatever is done to anyone is done to all - all or each, for we are one. This reminds me of a scripture attributed, I believe, to Jesus: *Whatsoever you do unto the least of these, my brethren, you do unto me.*

Wow! What power we have to build or to tear down for everyone is affected, and that means so am I. God give me grace, I pray, to chide in fairness and with kindness, if that is needed. And where 'tis possible, to lift in kind awareness.
Amen

Blessing in Adversity

Recently I had a luncheon date with three friends. It was a long time since we'd been together, but when we gathered in the same booth at a favorite restaurant we fell to talking like it had been yesterday. We perused the menu, made our choices, gave the server our requests and chattered like hens in a hen house until plates laden with attractive displays of food arrived. Before we 'dove in', one friend suggested a giving of thanks, to which we all happily agreed; we are all retired and live interesting lives, so have lots for which to be thankful. Health, happiness, abundance, security, and understanding mates or friends floated to the surface.

I was surprised, when it was my turn, that what I felt I was to give thanks for was adversity. I'd been going through a lot of that. And then it made so much sense. I had had peace through the adversities. The world had seemed to come falling down on me, but the love and light of God still shone through. I realized that adversity had given me the opportunity to find my own strength, joy and vision. The experience had given others a chance to see within me the 'peace that passes understanding'. Gradually the threads of adversity mended the fabric of life and I was ready for the next adventure. May we all similarly be blessed in adversity!

Hurrah! We All Win

Hurrah! I win, you win, we all win! We are catapulted into glory, into light and peace.

Loved ones gather round waiting for a turn to shake the hand of the one who has come out ahead... ahead of grumbling, sneering, rude gestures into the land where hearts are reconciled, where grudges and disparaging thought is washed away, where openness to holiness becomes the norm.

To some it may seem we've been devoured from the inside out, have succumbed to pain or have given in to lack of hope. To those in the 'know' the answer to our demise is quite different. We have chosen to move on to a different scene, to a new adventure.

Come along when you are ready, not a moment sooner, come into this place where all is pure and wholesome. Come here where we all win.

I Share with You

The little truth I have,
I have to share with you,
To leave with you for a time
When I'm absent, have bid adieu.

We are loved.
Yes, every one of us.
Accepted – wholeheartedly,
Understood, claimed, blessed.

Through rebellion,
Slackness, idiosyncrasies,
Forgetfulness and oddities
We are loved. Yes!

We claim, 'But I've done wrong,
I've cheated, told what wasn't true.
I've left undone the things
I knew I ought to do.'

'Welcome to the club.'
We have indeed.
It's part of the plan we set;
A plan upon which we agreed.

We have done what we said we would,
And played a difficult role.
Claim victory, for we see how this exercise
Has enlarged our souls.

Intention

The other day a friend complained about unfairness – he was frustrated about transactions regarding his taxes, and the seemingly botched transaction for which he'd paid good money. The unfortunate way things had been handled were eating him up.

The spirit of God spoke to him about letting go of the injustice and said he was to instead enjoy life as presented; his financial needs were met, family and friends were abundant, health was sound.

The message continued with encouragement to continue to do good; intention in matters was of greater significance than the facts and details.

Evidently we will be, and indeed are, already, blessed for the good intentions we have whether this involves us lending a hand or providing worldly materials. In the spiritual realm/heaven we are credited according to our intentions.

Well... I guess this means a lesson for me too.

Father/Mother/Sister/Brother/Friend thank you for this truth; help me, I pray, use this knowledge by endeavoring always to work from my higher consciousness.

Is It Worth It?

Harken. What do you hear?

I hear the laments of two soldiers. Each has lost a son in heavy fighting. They are distraught. Tears course their cheeks. They hang their heads in sorrow groaning without, aching within.

As evening descends they regroup with comrades on two sides of a useless storm of bullets and digitally directed warring devices.

Before dawn they have seen to further bereavements in several families.

People, is it worth it?

Recipe for Kindness

1 cup of truth
1 cup of gentleness and fond regard
2 tablespoons of thoughtfulness
1 ½ teaspoons restraint
Kindness, stirred in lightly

Sprinkle liberally with love
Eliminate judgment

Bake at 325⁰ for 45 minutes
Baste with a blend of acceptance and understanding

Serve to all whose lives you touch.

Build or Tear Down

Today a young man smiled and chattered cheerfully as he helped with bags of groceries. His pleasant disposition cheered me and healed us all.

The hairdresser untangled concerns and pain of her despondent client, while cutting, fashioning hair. In doing so she untangled pains of many.
Another soul dropped everything to lend a hand to fallen friend. We all were lifted.

The graciousness of thoughtful speech enlightened me. We all became much lighter. But when frustrated driver let go with a mouth of rage and gutter talk, we all were dissed.

Whatever is done to anyone is done to all - all or each, for we are one. This reminds me of a scripture attributed, I believe, to Jesus: *Whatsoever you do unto the least of these, my brethren, you do unto me.*

Wow! What power we have to build or to tear down for everyone is affected, and that means so am I. God give me grace, I pray, to chide in fairness and with kindness, if that is needed. And where 'tis possible, to lift in kind awareness. Amen

Blessing in Adversity

Recently I had a luncheon date with three friends. It was a long time since we'd been together, but when we gathered in the same booth at a favorite restaurant we fell to talking like it had been yesterday.

We perused the menu, made our choices, gave the server our requests and chattered like hens in a hen house until plates laden with attractive displays of food arrived. Before we 'dove in', one friend suggested a giving of thanks, to which we all happily agreed; we are all retired and live interesting lives, so have lots for which to be thankful. Health, happiness, abundance, security, and understanding mates or friends floated to the surface.

I was surprised, when it was my turn, that what I felt I was to give thanks for was adversity. I'd been going through a lot of that.

And then it made so much sense. I had had peace through the adversities. The world had seemed to come falling down on me, but the love and light of God still shone through. I realized that adversity had given me the opportunity to find my own strength, joy and vision. The experience had given others a chance to see within me the 'peace that passes understanding'. Gradually the threads of adversity mended the fabric of life and I was ready for the next adventure.

May we all similarly be blessed in adversity!

Best of Times/Worst of Times

Terrible times and wonderful times both hover on the horizon. A shift in actions will lead to a shift in thought. Even as seen in global hot spots today, so will we, too, experience terror and unrest – the worst of mankind.

We will also see generosity, thoughtfulness, acceptance and kindness explode. When darkness descends, wait patiently for the light.

Do not fear death – there is no such thing. Fear instead your lack of understanding of how Spirit operates and how the universe unwinds. Be at one with the sun, the sea, the bird in flight. Coo with the pigeon, call with raven. Allow spirit to lift you up above the heaviness of Earth.

How should we react in days to come? Fear not. Loud noises and flashing lights may appear. Stay calm, carry on. You have generations of loved ones who will take up your 'case' and help you find a way through. Welcome their suggestions, bask in their care and infinite love.

About the 'unwinding universe' – a lot of what we see and will see has already transpired. It has been captured in timelessness and is available in the 'now' which is where you live. Make what you can of this, it is hard to find words to do it justice.

Don't Worry. Be Thankful

There seem to be all kinds of things that could make us fret or worry; say 'be gone' to all of them. Instead of worrying, be thankful.

List your blessings, the times you've been a part of 'a miracle', the goodness that surrounds you, the love that is ever near. Give God, as you know him/her, appreciation for the strength you have, the lessons you have learned, the direction you've received.

You have a need? Be specific. Ask and see it materialize. I mean it, 'ask'! There is a scripture somewhere – *you have not because you ask not.* So, ask. Then remember to give thanks when your request is answered.

I told a friend the other day 'I'm not really as smart as I sometimes seem to be. It just looks like it because I go to the source that knows all, and ask'. I put even small concerns before God. Lot's of them begin "Where did I put____". (You name it.) Could be the toothpaste or my purse. Then I do as my mother coached, I just put my hand/s to whatever seems to need doing. In the scenario, the wayward item eventually comes to the surface, I am in peace, Spirit receives my grateful thanks and I look good. (I think this 'thanks' part is really important.} Lotsa luck!

Despair

In your life you may come across despair. The sky is dark and hangs low. Light escapes vision, the body is clothed in anguish, the mind dips into negative thinking – there seems to be no way out. Not so. The Spirit some may know as God is near, ready to take your hand and lead you into gladness.

You though must do your part. You need to put aside discouragement and pain, selfishness and wrath.

Search for the light within, allow it to shine. At first that light might be sporadic and lack intensity, however as you turn from negative thinking you'll begin to see the reason/s behind the cloud you find yourself in; you'll learn the lessons you've been shown and you'll choose a new and better path.

You have been reaping what you sowed.

Make a commitment to seek your higher power, to fashion life based on love. Your intention alone will give you hope; you'll be shown a better path to walk. Do good, harm not: see spiritual and physical well-being become yours. Despair will have quietly evaporated and in its place you'll have found peace and good will.

Coasting

Down the hill we swooped on anything that resembled a sled. The feathered environment presented a rare opportunity in our coastal part of the globe. The white world enticed me and my siblings into boots, jackets and caps. Mittens were harder to find but we made 'do' even if had to borrow Dad's thick work socks.

We hugged and puffed as we trudged the hilly climb – then we'd whoop with glee as we went coasting down the hill, hanging on for 'dear life' when we hit the lumps and bumps. We'd shake ourselves off, then trudge uphill so we could once again whistle down the slope.

The philosopher in me applies the principles learned here to aspects of my life on earth; don't be surprised is you see me huffing and puffing at difficult times but then laughing with glee when I get a chance to coast. How about you?

Forgive

Who are you to withhold forgiveness or pardon from another? Meting justice is not your role. What makes you the harbinger of holiness?

You know that 'what goes around comes around' so surrender those harsh thoughts and ways?

It is not the harm another caused which holds you back; it is the hardness of your heart. Consider instead the reality of *'what you reap is what you sowed'*. Then act accordingly

S/he who has incurred your wrath will be challenged by the 'powers that be' if indeed s/he had wicked intention. That is not your call.

It is your job to leave the 'justice' you desire to the Great Spirit, to the one you may, perhaps, call God. Instead, be thankful for the life you have, the goodness you find follows you. Receive, indeed, the glories of your days.

Forgetfulness

Be forgetful of harm done by others, or words that cut you to the quick. Do not be mindful of recollections that pull you into mire. Release the hatred that these thoughts inspire.

Likewise forgive self, and toss into forgetfulness the negative things you may have said or done. In this moment you are loved, and ever were you, are you, shall you be.

Know this – I also love the souls that harmed you. I've forgiven them, God says, even as I forgave and forgive you.

There is naught that you can say or do that will make me change my mind. But know this – you live with what you say and do – it dwells within your shell.

So speak softly and with kindness, let honesty prevail. Be at one with the Spirit which is in us all and you'll do well.

Hey! We'll all do well.
Blessings!

Falling Down

We are responsible for what we say, what we do. Nobody 'made you do it'. If we make mistakes we have to face the consequences.

Pick yourself up, apologize, make amends, and set new goals for your understanding and patience. Learn and love. Seek grace.

Ask for wisdom in dealing with 'troubles' of various kinds. Respond with heart, and with gentleness. When you do this you move along the spiritual 'thermometer'; you will see that you are making progress in becoming more and more the being that you set out to be.

See the areas in which you progress and those that need strengthening. Give thanks for the teaching received and continue with gladness.

Earth School

That great spirit, the all-in-all that we may know as Father, Mother, Sister, Brother, Cousin, Friend, the All-in-All, God, realizes that we live in a difficult realm. S/he knows we are spiritual beings having an earthly experience. We have left the light and love of our real home to spend time on the dense planet known as Earth.

Yet, abide here awhile. Experience the 'magic' of the wind on your face, of rain enlivening your soul. See the changes found in nature on this planet through the seasons. Partake of the taste and aromas of its fruits.

Examine how the people live. Learn what works and what doesn't. Embrace that which is good for all. Aim high. You want to pass with more than a C+.

Sing. Dance. Explore. Do good. Bless and harm not. Deliver only truth yet operate in kindness.

Remember: you are the teacher as well as the student.

Forgetfulness

Be forgetful of harm done by others, or words that cut you to the quick. Do not be mindful of recollections that pull you into mire. Release the hatred that these thoughts inspire.

Likewise forgive self, and toss into forgetfulness the negative things you may have said or done. In this moment you are loved, and ever were you, are you, shall you be.

Know this – I also love the souls that harmed you. I've forgiven them, God says, even as I forgave and forgive you.

There is naught that you can say or do that will make me change my mind. But know this – you live with what you say and do – it dwells within your shell.

So speak softly and with kindness, let honesty prevail. Be at one with the Spirit which is in us all and you'll do well.

Hey! We'll all do well.
Blessings!

Forgive

Who are you to withhold forgiveness or pardon from another? Meting justice is not your role. What makes you the harbinger of holiness?

You know that 'what goes around comes around' so surrender those harsh thoughts and ways?

It is not the harm another caused which holds you back; it is the hardness of your heart. Consider instead the reality of *'what you reap is what you sowed'*. Then act accordingly

S/he who has incurred your wrath will be challenged by the 'powers that be' if indeed s/he had wicked intention. That is not your call.

It is your job to leave the 'justice' you desire to the Great Spirit, to the one you may, perhaps, call God. Instead, be thankful for the life you have, the goodness you find follows you. Receive, indeed, the glories of your days.

Graduation

Though I have not yet completed all the course work, I know I have already graduated! Come, graduate with me.

Some time ago God gave me to understand, that when this life ends and I next transition from body, I need not have another life on earth. I may, if I wish; but if I'm ready, I can return to Source being once again, there, a God spark.

Because I've been used to having a body in the many lives I know I've lived, I must admit I was reluctant at first. The idea took some time for me to grasp and longer still for me to agree to it. However, I now embrace the plan. I'll return, in time, to be part of the All-in-All, taking with me the energy and experiences that here have been mine. This will be my 'graduation', and my graduation has already been declared. Whoopee!

Unless I'm taken soon, that celebration will have to wait for I've an inclination there's quite a list of 'more to do' waiting on my plate. Until that list appears I'll relax, for soon I'll see what Spirit has in store for me.

Please wish me well :) M

Greed

Greed has many faces: could be the last chocolate in the box or stealing the limelight. Could be selling useless 'goods' or flogging mindless 'opportunities'.

There is nothing wrong with wanting to 'get ahead' or to provide for family. However, do not do this at a brother's expense or by causing a sister harm.

The goodness of the one we know as God loves the buyer as much as the seller, the carpenter as much as the king. If you 'steal' from another, you steal from self for you are your brother, your sister – we are one.

What 'goes around, 'comes around'. Therefore be generous and thoughtful, wise, fair and kind. See these attributes amplified descending on you.

Yet do not 'good' only because of repercussions, but do good as a practice of right living.

Accept a gift of wisdom from Spirit so that you might know what to keep and what to give, what to lend and when to borrow. Be blessed as you put greed behind you and fair play ahead.

Hinder Not

Harm not, nor hinder growth.

Who am I, who are you, to harm another?

Would you have what you exhibit come back with force upon you?

What goes around comes around is a law of the planet – you witness this time and time again.

Therefore harm not. And hinder not the growth of another.

Hold One Another Together

Without the grace of God we are naught.
If the sun doesn't shine nor the rain fall,
what will you eat but one another?

If the rivers dry up wild beast will claim
you, the ravens will pick your bones.

Seek grace, seek the source – the all-in-all,
the Holy Spirit that you may know as God.

A spark of that spirit is within each,
but a spark, does not God make.

Therefore do not think too highly of self.
*but see yourself as a building stone in a
monument, not alone, but holding one another
together, giving refuge to the souls of man.*

Greeted in the Morning

Who is this that awakens with me so early in the morning?

Ah, it is the spirit of gladness that greets me, and it is the consciousness of longevity, of wisdom, and of goodness.

Eat wisely, be aware, deliver peace even in difficult moments.

You are a book others read, a beacon of light when darkness crowds near. Who you are has more effect than what you say. Therefore let laughter tumble from your lips, encouragement be the key that opens every door.

Spread love in great abandon on the feet of those whose path you cross. Soak up the joy that's offered, be a mirror of the same. Yet weep with those who cry, whose hope has turned to dust, envelope them in love. Be near. Be kind.

How Can We Reunite as One, I Ask?

Spirit responds - 'you are one, we are one'.

There is no 'reuniting' to be done. What is needed is that you open your eyes, ears and hearts to the oneness that you be.

You may see yourself as separate – wearing different garments, singing different songs. I say – you are one. The consciousness of all flows together, is intermingled leaving all to reap the pain or blessings of this unity, this oneness that you be.

When raindrops fall into the sea do they keep their identity, or do they meld with those gone before? Can you separate the drop of 'now' from the pool of 'then'? Of course you cannot.

Like-wise are you in this sea of nations and nationalities, one. One. Now and always.

The differences you see are cosmetic. The similarities, profound. In love grasp the hand offered, recognize the smile displayed. Start a chain reaction of acceptance and good deeds.

Amen.

Hurrah! We All Win

Hurrah! I win, you win, we all win! We are catapulted into glory, into light and peace.

Loved ones gather round waiting for a turn to shake the hand of the one who has come out ahead... ahead of grumbling, sneering, rude gestures into the land where hearts are reconciled, where grudges and disparaging thought is washed away, where openness to holiness becomes the norm.

To some it may seem we've been devoured from the inside out, have succumbed to pain or have given in to lack of hope. To those in the 'know' the answer to our demise is quite different. We have chosen to move on to a different scene, to a new adventure.

Come along when you are ready, not a moment sooner, come into this place where all is pure and wholesome. Come here where we all win.

I Share with You

The little truth I have,
I have to share with you,
To leave with you for a time
When I'm absent, have bid adieu.

We are loved.
Yes, every one of us.
Accepted – wholeheartedly,
Understood, claimed, blessed.

Through rebellion,
Slackness, idiosyncrasies,
Forgetfulness and oddities
We are loved. Yes!

We claim, 'But I've done wrong,
I've cheated, told what wasn't true.
I've left undone the things
I knew I ought to do.'

'Welcome to the club.'
We have indeed.
It's part of the plan we set;
A plan upon which we agreed.

We have done what we said we would,
And played a difficult role.
Claim victory, for we see how this exercise
Has enlarged our souls.

Intention

The other day a friend complained about unfairness – he was frustrated about transactions regarding his taxes, and the seemingly botched transaction for which he'd paid good money. The unfortunate way things had been handled were eating him up.

The spirit of God spoke to him about letting go of the injustice and said he was to instead enjoy life as presented; his financial needs were met, family and friends were abundant, health was sound.

The message continued with encouragement to continue to do good; intention in matters was of greater significance than the facts and details.

Evidently we will be, and indeed are, already, blessed for the good intentions we have whether this involves us lending a hand or providing worldly materials. In the spiritual realm/heaven we are credited according to our intentions.

Well... I guess this means a lesson for me too.

Father/Mother/Sister/Brother/Friend thank you for this truth; help me, I pray, use this knowledge by endeavoring always to work from my higher consciousness.

Is It Worth It?

Harken. What do you hear?

I hear the laments of two soldiers. Each has lost a son in heavy fighting. They are distraught. Tears course their cheeks. They hang their heads in sorrow groaning without, aching within.

As evening descends they regroup with comrades on two sides of a useless storm of bullets and digitally directed warring devices.

Before dawn they have seen to further bereavements in several families.

People, is it worth it?

Recipe for Kindness

1 cup of truth
1 cup of gentleness and fond regard
2 tablespoons of thoughtfulness
1 ½ teaspoons restraint
Kindness, stirred in lightly

Sprinkle liberally with love
Eliminate judgment

Bake at 325⁰ for 45 minutes
Baste with a blend of acceptance and understanding

Serve to all whose lives you touch.

Printed in the United States
By Bookmasters